A LOOK AT EARTH'S ROCKS

WHAT ARE IGNEOUS ROCKS?

BY KRISTEN RAJCZAK NELSON

Gareth Stevens PUBLISHING

CRASHCOURSE

Please visit our website, www.garethstevens.com. For a free color catalog of all our high-quality books, call toll free 1-800-542-2595 or fax 1-877-542-2596.

Cataloging-in-Publication Data

Names: Nelson, Kristen Rajczak.
Title: What are igneous rocks? / Kristen Rajczak Nelson.
Description: New York : Gareth Stevens Publishing, 2018. | Series: A look at earth's rocks | Includes index.
Identifiers: ISBN 9781482462531 (pbk.) | ISBN 9781482462548 (library bound) | ISBN 9781482462524 (6 pack)
Subjects: LCSH: Igneous rocks--Juvenile literature.
Classification: LCC QE461.N45 2018 | DDC 552'.1--dc23

First Edition

Published in 2018 by
Gareth Stevens Publishing
111 East 14th Street, Suite 349
New York, NY 10003

Designer: Samantha DeMartin
Editor: Kristen Nelson

Photo credits: Series background winnond/Shutterstock.com; caption box Edhar Shvets/Shutterstock.com; cover, p. 1 Anna Azimi/Shutterstock.com; p. 5 (top) Linda M. Foster/Shutterstock.com; pp. 5 (bottom), 21 Artography/Shutterstock.com; p. 7 (earth) Lukiyanova Natalia/Shutterstock.com; p. 7 (sky) Kichigin/Shutterstock.com; p. 9 MarcelClemens/Shutterstock.com; p. 11 Ronn Hook/Shutterstock.com; p. 13 (top) Zack Frank/Shutterstock.com; p. 13 (bottom) Visuals Unlimited, Inc./Marli Miller/Visuals Unlimited/Getty Images; p. 15 Handout/Getty Images News/Getty Images; p. 17 Irina Moss/Shutterstock.com; p. 19 kavram/Shutterstock.com; p. 23 (main) photolike/Shutterstock.com; p. 23 (inset) vvoe/Shutterstock.com; p. 25 (coarse-grained) De Agostini/A. Rizzi/De Agostini Picture Library/Getty Images; p. 25 (volcanic glass) Giovanna Di Maruo/Shutterstock.com; p. 25 (fine-grained) Michael C. Rygel/Wikimedia Commons; p. 27 (top) Four Oaks/Shutterstock.com; p. 27 (bottom) valeriiaamaud/Shutterstock.com; p. 29 Westend61/Getty Images; p. 30 Carlyn Iverson/Science Source/Getty Images.

Printed in the United States of America

CPSIA compliance information: Batch #CS17GS: For further information contact Gareth Stevens, New York, New York at 1-800-542-2595.

CONTENTS

Words in the glossary appear in **bold** type the first time they are used in the text.

HOT ROCK

Much of Earth is made of igneous rock. This rock began as hot, liquid rock deep underground. Often, we can't even see it forming! Igneous rock is one of the three main kinds of rock found on Earth.

MAKE THE GRADE

The other two types of rock are **metamorphic** rock and **sedimentary** rock.

Hot, liquid rock inside Earth is called magma. It can reach 1,100 to 2,400°F (600 to 1,300°C)! Magma is found starting about 40 miles (64 km) below Earth's surface. It includes **molten** rock called the melt, **mineral** crystals, gases, and some solid rock.

EARTH'S LAYERS

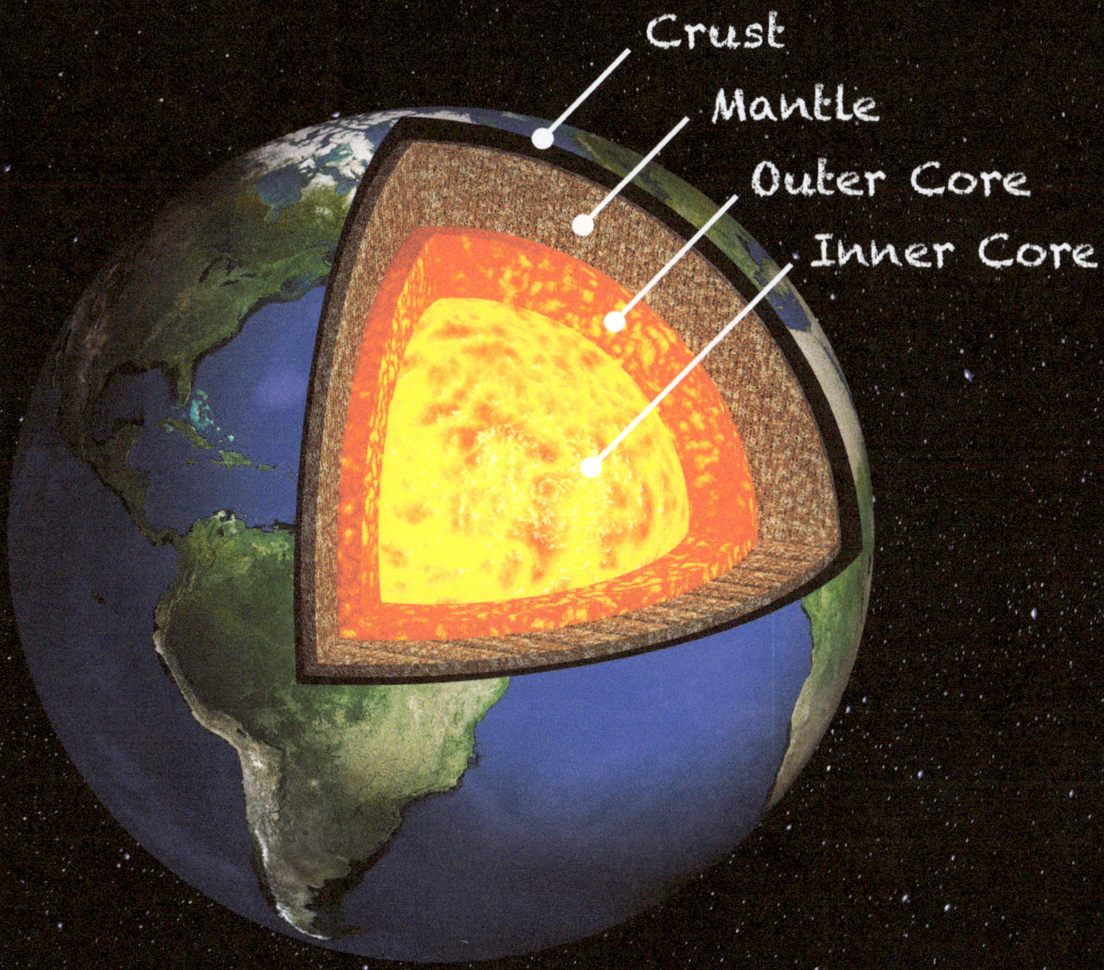

MAKE THE GRADE

Earth is divided into four layers. Magma forms in the upper part of the mantle and the lower part of the top layer, the crust.

Magma that reaches Earth's surface as a liquid is called lava. Igneous rock forms when magma or lava cools. This often happens as magma moves toward Earth's surface. Magma tends to rise because it's less **dense** than the rock around it.

MAKE THE GRADE

Most liquid rock is studied as lava. It's hard to find magma that hasn't reached the surface yet!

INTRUSIVE

There are two types of igneous rock. When magma cools into rock underground, it forms intrusive igneous rock. Intrusive igneous rock often forms where magma pools in small open spaces or tunnels beneath Earth's surface.

MAKE THE GRADE

Magma cools slowly underground when forming intrusive igneous rock.

The tunnels intrusive igneous rocks form in can make them look like thick plant roots. Some intrusive rocks are small. They can also form into huge **domes** that cover more than 40 square miles (104 sq km).

MAKE THE GRADE

The core, or innermost part, of some mountain ranges is made up of intrusive igneous rock.

SIERRA NEVADA

INTRUSIVE IGNEOUS ROCK

EXTRUSIVE

Extrusive igneous rock forms when magma reaches Earth's surface as lava and cools. Magma escapes through cracks in Earth's crust called volcanoes. The lava that forms extrusive igneous rock cools very quickly.

MAKE THE GRADE

Volcanoes are any cracks in Earth's crust where lava and hot gases flow out.

Many volcanoes look like mountains. Extrusive igneous rock builds up over time from volcanic **eruptions**. When a volcano erupts, it may shoot molten rock out of its top. That means extrusive igneous rock can also form far from an active volcano.

MAKE THE GRADE

As lava flows around a volcano, it forms sheets of extrusive igneous rock called a lava field.

INSIDE IGNEOUS ROCK

All igneous rock is made up of minerals. However, only the slow cooling of intrusive igneous rock allows these minerals to "grow." That means the minerals form crystals! How the crystals look helps scientists figure out what mineral they are.

MAKE THE GRADE

Extrusive igneous rock cools so quickly minerals don't have time to form crystals.

How igneous rock forms affects what it looks like. The different minerals found in igneous rock also play a part in a rock's appearance. Igneous rock can be white, pink, gray, black, or brown, depending on the minerals in it.

MAKE THE GRADE

Intrusive and extrusive igneous rocks form from the same magma—yet they can look so different!

Igneous rocks are grouped by the amount of the mineral silica in them. Felsic igneous rocks have the most silica at 66 percent or more. Ultramafic igneous rocks have the least amount of silica in them at 45 percent or less.

MAKE THE GRADE

Felsic igneous rock is often light colored. But one type of felsic igneous rock, called obsidian, is black or dark brown.

OBSIDIAN

FINE OR COARSE?

Igneous rocks can have different **textures** from one another, too. Extrusive igneous rock tends to be fine **grained** since it cooled so quickly when it formed. Intrusive igneous rock, which cooled slower, is often **coarse** grained.

MAKE THE GRADE

When lava cools instantly, it looks like glass, but is still a kind of extrusive igneous rock.

FINE-GRAINED EXTRUSIVE

VOLCANIC GLASS

COARSE-GRAINED INTRUSIVE

GRANITE AND BASALT

Two well-known kinds of igneous rock show how different these rocks may be. Granite is light-colored and coarse-grained. Basalt is commonly black and may be very smooth or look somewhat like a sponge.

MAKE THE GRADE

Scientists often use texture, color, and other features of a rock to **identify** it.

GRANITE

BASALT

NEW ROCK

Igneous rocks are an important part of the rock cycle. Any kind of rock can become molten deep underground. Later, that molten rock returns to Earth's surface, sometimes as islands that form above underwater volcanoes. New igneous rock forms all the time!

MAKE THE GRADE

The rock cycle is the model used to show how rock forms, breaks down, and forms again over time.

HOW DOES IGNEOUS ROCK FORM?

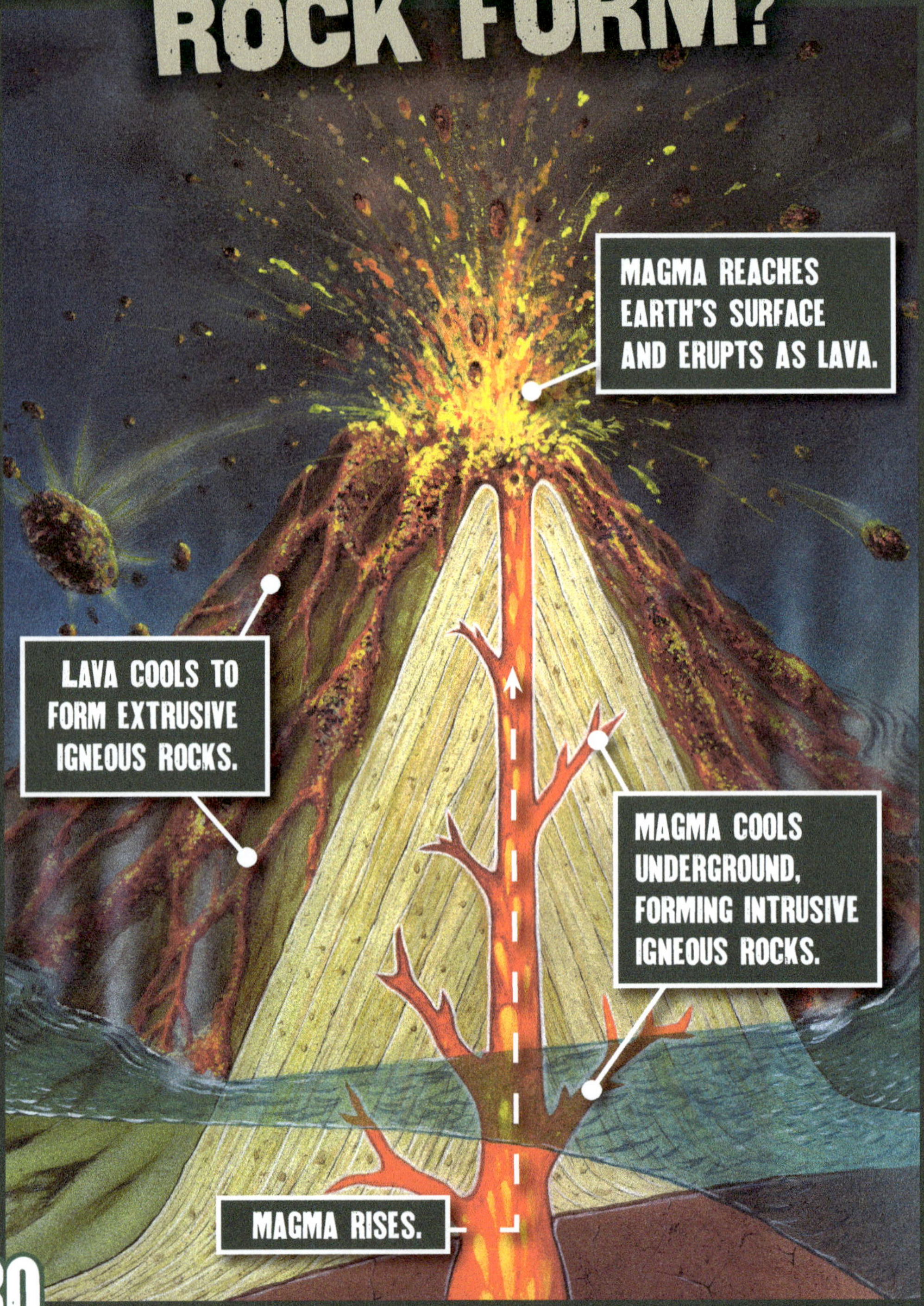

GLOSSARY

coarse: being made up of large pieces

dense: having matter packed tightly together in a given area

dome: a rounded shape that looks like half a ball

eruption: the bursting forth of hot, liquid rock from within Earth

grained: having to do with the size of the mineral grains that make up a rock

identify: to find out the name or features of something

metamorphic: having to do with rock that has been changed by temperature, pressure, or other natural forces

mineral: matter in the ground that forms rocks

molten: changed into a liquid form by heat

sedimentary: having to do with rock that forms when sand, stones, and other matter are pressed together over a long time

texture: in the study of rocks, the size of a mineral's crystals or grains in the rock

FOR MORE INFORMATION

BOOKS

Brannon, Cecelia H. *A Look at Igneous Rocks*. New York, NY: Enslow Publishing, 2016.

Lindeen, Mary. *Investigating the Rock Cycle*. Minneapolis, MN: Lerner Publications, 2016.

WEBSITES

Igneous Rocks
onegeology.org/extra/kids/igneous.html
Review how igneous rocks form on this website.

The Rock Cycle
eschooltoday.com/rocks/the-rock-cycle.html
Find out more about how rocks change over time.

Publisher's note to educators and parents: Our editors have carefully reviewed these websites to ensure that they are suitable for students. Many websites change frequently, however, and we cannot guarantee that a site's future contents will continue to meet our high standards of quality and educational value. Be advised that students should be closely supervised whenever they access the Internet.

INDEX